LET'S FIND OUT! RELIGION

ISLAM

TAYYABA SYED

Britannica®
Educational Publishing

IN ASSOCIATION WITH

ROSEN
EDUCATIONAL SERVICES

Published in 2019 by Britannica Educational Publishing (a trademark of Encyclopædia Britannica, Inc.) in association with The Rosen Publishing Group, Inc.
29 East 21st Street, New York, NY 10010

Distributed exclusively by Rosen Publishing.
To see additional Britannica Educational Publishing titles, go to rosenpublishing.com.

First Edition

Britannica Educational Publishing
J.E. Luebering: Executive Director, Core Editorial
Mary Rose McCudden: Editor, Britannica Student Encyclopedia

Rosen Publishing
Jacob R. Steinberg: Editor
Nicole Russo-Duca: Series Designer and Book Layout
Cindy Reiman: Photography Manager
Nicole DiMella: Photo Researcher

Library of Congress Cataloging-in-Publication Data

Names: Syed, Tayyaba, author.
Title: Islam / Tayyaba Syed.
Description: New York : Britannica Educational Publishing, in Association with Rosen Educational Services, 2019 | Series: Let's find out! Religion | Includes bibliographical references and index. | Audience: Grades 1–5.
Identifiers: LCCN 2018014132 | ISBN 9781508106869 (library bound) | ISBN 9781508107170 (pbk.) | ISBN 9781508107286 (6 pack)
Subjects: LCSH: Islam—Juvenile literature. | Islam—Doctrines—Juvenile literature. | Muslims—Juvenile literature.
Classification: LCC BP161.3 .S94 2019 | DDC 297—dc23
LC record available at https://lccn.loc.gov/2018014132
Manufactured in the United States of America

Photo credits: Cover and interior pages background Ahmad Faizal Yahya/Moment/Getty Images; p. 4 TonyV3112/Shutterstock.com; p. 5 © Encyclopædia Britannica, Inc.; p. 6 Art Directors & TRIP/Alamy Stock Photo; p. 7 David Lazar/Moment Select/Getty Images; p. 8 Arthur Tilley/Stockbyte/Getty Images; p. 9 © Ingo Jezierski/Getty Images; p. 10 Sapsiwai/Shutterstock.com; p. 11 DEA Picture Library/De Agostini/Getty Images; p. 12 Topkapi Palace Museum, Istanbul, Turkey/© Luisa Ricciarini/Leemage/Bridgeman Images; p. 13 artpixelgraphy Studio/Shutterstock.com; p. 14 The Madina Collection of Islamic Art, gift of Camilla Chandler Frost/Los Angeles County Museum of Art; pp. 15, 18 © Photos.com/Thinkstock; p. 16 Fayez Nureldine/AFP/Getty Images; p. 17 Atta Kenare/AFP/Getty Images; p. 19 Gerard Sioen/Gamma-Rapho/Getty Images; p. 20 © Fuse/Thinkstock; p. 21 Noorullah Shirzada/AFP/Getty Images; p. 22 NurPhoto/Getty Images; p. 23 Khaled Desouki/AFP/Getty Images; p. 24 © ayazad/Fotolia; p. 25 Ahmad Gharabli/AFP/Getty Images; p. 26 DEA/V. Pirozzi/ De Agostini/Getty Images; p. 27 Francois Lochon/Gamma-Rapho/Getty Images; p. 28 Max Milligan/AWL Images/Getty Images; p. 29 Maskot/Getty Images.

CONTENTS

WHAT IS ISLAM?

Islam is one of the world's major religions. It was founded in the seventh century CE by Muhammad in what is now Saudi Arabia. Followers of Islam are called Muslims.

Like Christianity and Judaism, Islam is monotheistic. It teaches that there is only one God, called Allah, and that he created the world. The Arabic word "Islam" means "submission" or "surrender." Muslims strive to live a life obeying the will of Allah.

Muslims pray in a mosque in Yinchuan, China.

4

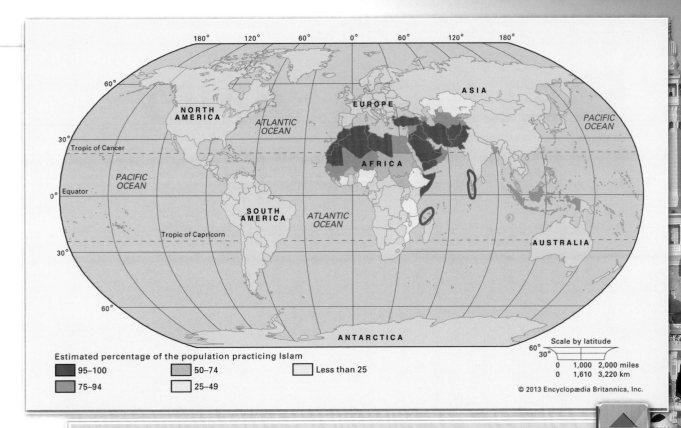

Estimated percentage of the population practicing Islam

- 95–100
- 75–94
- 50–74
- 25–49
- Less than 25

Scale by latitude
60°
30°

| 0 | 1,000 | 2,000 miles |
| 0 | 1,610 | 3,220 km |

© 2013 Encyclopædia Britannica, Inc.

This map shows the world distribution of Islam. Darker green countries have a higher percentage of Muslims.

Today, Islam is the second largest religion in the world. It has about 1.6 billion followers worldwide, or one-fifth of the world's population. Most Muslims live in North Africa, the Middle East, and southern and central Asia.

BELIEFS AND PRACTICES

At the center of Islam is this statement of faith, called the *shahadah*: "There is no God but Allah, and Muhammad is the prophet of Allah." It states the oneness of God and the belief that Muhammad was the last prophet in a long line of prophets. Muslims believe that God is kind and fair and that God created the world

VOCABULARY

A **prophet** is a religious messenger. This person shares a message that he or she believes has come from God with other people.

The shahadah appears in Arabic above the entrance to a mosque.

Muslims pray at five specific times each day, often in mosques but also sometimes in markets or other public places.

and will one day judge humankind. They believe that the Koran, the holy book of Islam, is the word of God as told to Muhammad.

Muslims practice their faith not just as a religion but also as a way of life. Five duties, called the five pillars of Islam, are expected of every Muslim. The first pillar, the shahadah, or statement of faith, is the most important.

The second pillar of Islam is prayer. Muslims pray five times a day: at dawn, midday, midafternoon, sunset, and before going to bed. Before prayer, Muslims wash

Modern mosques often have loudspeakers to project the call to prayer to nearby people.

their hands, feet, and face. A person called the muezzin calls for prayers and chants from a raised platform or minaret tower at the mosque, the place of worship. A person called the imam stands at the front of the mosque facing Mecca, the holy city of Islam, and leads the congregation in prayer. The congregation lines up in rows behind the imam. There are no seats in a mosque. During prayer, Muslims stand, kneel, and bow down. On Fridays, communities gather at the mosque for special prayers. They pray, listen to parts of the Koran, and hear a sermon.

The third pillar of Islam is charity, or money given to the poor and needy of the community. The fourth pillar is to fast, or go without food, from sunrise to sunset during the holy month of Ramadan. The fifth pillar is to make a pilgrimage to the holy city of Mecca in Saudi Arabia at least once.

THINK ABOUT IT

Why do you think Muslims face Mecca when they pray?

Mosques are important centers of Islam. This mosque in the Southeast Asian country of Brunei is known for its beauty.

WHO WAS MUHAMMAD?

Muhammad, the founder of Islam, was born in the Arabian town of Mecca in about 570 CE. Muhammad's father died before he was born, and Muhammad's mother died when he was six. He was raised by his grandfather and later by his uncle. Muhammad grew up poor but worked very hard. First he worked as a shepherd. Later he became a well-known tradesman.

When Muhammad was about twenty-five years old, he married a rich, older woman named Khadijah. Their marriage helped Muhammad

Today, Mecca is a large city that receives many tourists every year.

This thirteenth-century drawing shows Mecca, which was visited by Muslim pilgrims even then.

become wealthy and important in his community. Muhammad and Khadijah had six children. Two of their sons died when they were young. Of their four daughters, the best known is Fatima. Although many men at the time had more than one wife, Khadijah was Muhammad's only wife until she died. After her death, he took several wives.

THINK ABOUT IT

One of the five pillars of Islam is charity for the poor. Do you think the circumstances of Muhammad's life may have influenced this duty? Why or why not?

Muhammad received his first message from God through the angel Gabriel, whom he saw in a vision.

From time to time, Muhammad climbed a mountain near Mecca. There, he would sit in a cave to **meditate**. One night in the year 610 CE, Muhammad was in this cave when he received what he believed was a message from God. Muhammad had a vision of the angel Gabriel, who told Muhammad there was one God, not many gods, as most Arabs believed. The angel also told Muhammad that Allah had chosen him as a prophet.

VOCABULARY

To **meditate** means to spend time in quiet thinking or reflecting.

12

Throughout his life, Muhammad continued to receive messages that he believed came from God. In about 613 Muhammad began preaching the new ideas that had been revealed to him. Many people in Mecca were against the new ideas. Muhammad worried that his enemies might hurt him and his followers. He encouraged his followers to move to the nearby city of Medina. Muhammad himself reached Medina on September 24, 622, which is considered the starting date for the history of Islam. Muhammad's trip to Medina is known as the Hegira.

Pilgrims enter the cave near Mecca where Muhammad received his first prophecy.

THE KORAN

Muhammad memorized the messages he received from God and recited them to his followers. His followers then wrote them down, and these writings became the Koran, the holy book of Islam. The word "Koran" is an English version of the Arabic word Qur'an, which means "recitation."

Muslims believe the answers to all religious, social, and legal issues are in the Koran. One important subject in the Koran is resurrection, or rising from the dead. Other topics include angels and devils, heaven and hell, and foods that are forbidden to eat,

The Koran contains 114 suras, or chapters, of various lengths. Each sura contains a prayer and verses. After the first sura, the suras are organized from longest to shortest.

All Muslims memorize short sections of the Koran to recite in their daily prayers. When it is recited, the Koran may sound like poetry or song.

such as pork. There are also chapters about marriage and divorce laws. Other sections tell the duties of parents to their children, of masters to their servants, and of the rich to the poor. The Koran also includes stories about prophets and people in the Bible.

COMPARE AND CONTRAST
How is the Koran similar to another religious text you know about, for example, the Christian Bible or the Torah of Judaism? How is the Koran different?

Muslims believe that everything Muhammad said and did was inspired by Allah. Because of that, his followers wrote down many of his words and actions. These writings, called Hadith, serve as an additional guide for Muslims, along with the Koran.

THE SPREAD OF ISLAM

Muhammad eventually persuaded most of the people of Arabia, including Mecca, to follow Islam. But after Muhammad's death in 632 CE, Muslims disagreed as to who should lead them. Muhammad's son-in-law 'Ali became the Muslim leader, or caliph, in 656. But he was murdered in 661. Some Muslims thought that 'Ali's descendants should be their leaders. This group formed the Shi'ah

Children in Saudi Arabia celebrate the country's National Day. Most Saudi Arabians are Sunnites.

branch of Islam and are called Shi'ites. The Muslims who disagreed formed the Sunnah branch.

Most Muslims are Sunnites, or followers of the Sunnah branch. They are known as traditional Muslims. They follow the sayings of Muhammad and emphasize community.

THINK ABOUT IT

Most of the world's religions have different branches or schools of thought. Why do you think this is?

Members of the smaller Shi'ah branch, called Shi'ites, believe that the truths of the Koran are revealed only through the imam. Interpretations by other people are not accepted. For this reason Shi'ites are not as open to other views as Sunnites are.

During the 600s and 700s, Islam spread far beyond Arabia, from the western Mediterranean region to Central Asia. Holy wars called jihads were fought to conquer new lands and spread Islam.

In the Middle East a group called the Seljuks would not let Christians visit holy sites in the land

The Crusades were a series of wars between Christians and Muslims for control of the Holy Land.

Istanbul, Turkey, has been an important center of Islamic culture since the time of the Ottoman Empire.

they controlled. Over the next two centuries, Muslims and Christians fought over the Holy Land in a series of wars known as the Crusades. In the 1200s another group of Muslim Turks, the Ottomans, began a powerful Islamic empire. The Ottomans eventually ruled over North Africa, the Middle East, and southeastern Europe for hundreds of years.

VOCABULARY

The **Holy Land** is a part of the Middle East that is sacred to three major religions: Judaism, Christianity, and Islam. It lies between the Jordan River and the Mediterranean Sea and includes the city of Jerusalem.

HOLIDAYS

The two major religious holidays in the Muslim calendar are 'Id al-Fitr and 'Id al-Adha. 'Id al-Fitr happens at the end of Ramadan. The ninth month of the Islamic calendar, Ramadan marks the time when Muhammad received the words of the Koran. Muslims observe Ramadan by praying, reading the Koran, and fasting. Muslims believe

COMPARE AND CONTRAST

Because the Islamic calendar is based on the moon, Ramadan may happen in any season of the year. Think about other holidays, such as Christmas or Passover. Do they always occur in the same season?

A young boy celebrates Ramadan, the holiest month of the year in Islam.

Young Afghan boys read from the Koran during the holy month of Ramadan.

their past sins will be forgiven if they participate in Ramadan.

During Ramadan, most Muslims must fast during daylight hours. Small children, old people, and sick people may eat. After sunset, Muslims break their fast with prayer and festive meals. Called *iftar*, these meals are shared with friends and family. After meals, people visit other friends and relatives. The twenty-seventh night of Ramadan is celebrated as the Night of Power, or Lailat al Kadr. On that night, it is said, God revealed the Koran. Muslims spend extra hours in prayer then.

When Ramadan ends, Muslims celebrate 'Id al-Fitr, or the Festival of Breaking Fast. 'Id al-Fitr occurs during the first three days of Shawwal, the tenth month of the Islamic calendar. Muslims begin the festival by praying together at dawn on the first day. Later, families gather to enjoy special meals and sweets. Children wear new clothes, and gifts are exchanged. People also visit the graves of relatives. Some cities hold large ceremonies outdoors.

The holiday 'Id al-Adha is held each year to mark the end of the hajj, the pilgrimage to Mecca. Its name means the Festival of Sacrifice. It commemorates a story in the Koran in which God asks Ibrahim (also known as Abraham) to sacrifice his son. Ibrahim prepares to do so, but then God lets him sacrifice a ram instead. 'Id al-Adha lasts for four days. It is a time for prayer, visiting with friends and family, and giving gifts. Some families sacrifice an animal and divide the meat among family members, friends, neighbors, and the poor.

COMPARE AND CONTRAST

How are the holidays of 'Id al-Fitr and 'Id al-Adha similar? How are they different?

23

THE HAJJ

The fifth pillar of Islam is the hajj—the pilgrimage that Muslims must make to Mecca, Saudi Arabia, in their lifetime. Hajj begins on the eighth day of Dhu al-Hijjah (the last month of the Islamic year) and ends on the thirteenth day. About two million people perform the hajj each year. Every Muslim who is physically and financially able must make the pilgrimage.

Before reaching Mecca, pilgrims enter a state of holiness and purity called ihram. In this state, pilgrims wear white and do

The Ka'bah is a cube shaped building. It is about 50 feet high (15 meters), and it is about 35 (11 m) by 40 (12 m) feet at its base. The Black Stone is built into the eastern wall of the Ka'bah.

not cut their hair or nails. When they reach Mecca, pilgrims walk seven times around a sacred shrine called the Ka'bah in the Great Mosque. They try to touch or kiss the Black Stone in the Ka'bah. Outside of Mecca, pilgrims visit the site of Muhammad's last sermon and ask God's forgiveness. It is the most important part of the hajj. At the end of the hajj, pilgrims return to Mecca and circle the Ka'bah again before leaving the city.

Muslims try to touch the Ka'bah during the hajj, or pilgrimage, to Mecca.

VOCABULARY

A **shrine** is a place or an object that is considered sacred, or holy.

Modern Islam

During the 1800s and 1900s Western powers established colonies in Muslim nations to trade with the people living there. Islamic leaders lost political power, but Muslims gathered together more tightly as a community in response to colonization. In the 1900s this sense of unity helped many Muslim countries fight for and win political independence.

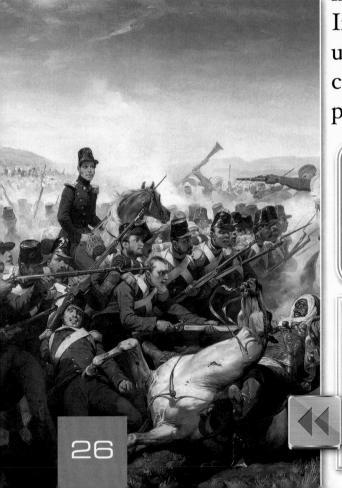

VOCABULARY
Colonization is the act of a nation taking control of a distant territory.

A painting shows a battle between French and Algerian troops. France took control of Muslim Algeria in the 1800s.

Ruhollah Khomeini was a political and religious leader of Iran. Khomeini's government enforced strict Muslim laws and banned Western influences.

In the late 1900s Islam became one of the fastest-growing world religions. Some Muslims have resisted the influence of the West, which they view as leading to a loss of traditional Muslim values. In Iran a revolution brought Islamic religious leaders to power in 1979. Today, Shi'ism is the national religion of Iran. Islam has had a strong influence on the governments of other countries as well.

Islam is the most popular religion in more than thirty countries. The world's mostly Muslim countries form a long band from the Atlantic Ocean across North Africa, the Middle East, and South and Central Asia. Indonesia, an island nation in the Indian and Pacific oceans, has more Muslims than any other country.

Muslims also live in other countries throughout the world. In the United States and Canada, there are more

Muslims form an important part of Western societies and local communities. ▶▶

than three million Muslims. Muslims in North America come from many different backgrounds. Despite the differences in their backgrounds, Muslims around the world view themselves as one community united in belief.

THINK ABOUT IT

How might the hajj help maintain the link between Muslims from all over the world?

Glossary

Arabia Peninsula of southwest Asia including Saudi Arabia, Yemen, Oman, and the Persian Gulf States.

chant To speak with little or no change in tone.

charity The giving of aid to the poor and suffering.

colonization The act of a nation taking control over a distant territory.

devout Having a strong belief in a religion.

fast To go without eating.

Holy Land Part of the Middle East that is sacred to Judaism, Christianity, and Islam and includes the city of Jerusalem.

minaret A tall tower of a mosque from which a muezzin calls worshipers to prayer.

memorize To learn by heart.

mosque A Muslim place of worship.

pillar A supporting or important part of something.

pilgrimage A journey to a shrine or holy place to worship.

prophet A person who shares a message that he or she believes has come from God.

sacrifice Killing an animal as an offering to God.

sermon A talk that teaches a lesson, usually given by a religious leader.

shrine A place or an object that is considered sacred or holy.

FOR MORE INFORMATION

Books

Al-Hassani, Salim. *1001 Inventions & Awesome Facts from Muslim Civilization.* Washington DC: National Geographic Society, 2012.

Ali-Karamali, Sumbal. *Growing Up Muslim.* New York, NY: Random House, 2012.

Brown, Tricia. *Salaam: A Muslim American Boy's Story.* New York, NY: Henry Holt and Company, 2006.

Petrini, Catherine M. *What Makes Me a Muslim?* Farmington Hills, MI: KidHaven Press, 2005.

Wood, Angela. *Muslim Mosque.* Milwaukee, WI: Gareth Stevens Publishing, 2000.

Websites

BBC
www.bbc.co.uk/schools/religion/islam/

United Religions Initiative
https://uri.org/kids/world-religions/muslim-beliefs

World Religions for Kids
https://kids.kiddle.co/Islam

INDEX